MW01536865

"Hey Big Head"

"Hey Big Head"

❧

Curtis Yarborough

Copyright © 2011 by Curtis Yarborough.

Library of Congress Control Number:		2011904764
ISBN:	Hardcover	978-1-4568-6381-4
	Softcover	978-1-4568-6380-7
	Ebook	978-1-4568-6382-1

All rights reserved. No part of this book may be reproduced or transmitted in any form or by any means, electronic or mechanical, including photocopying, recording, or by any information storage and retrieval system, without permission in writing from the copyright owner.

This book was printed in the United States of America.

To order additional copies of this book, contact:
Xlibris Corporation
1-888-795-4274
www.Xlibris.com
Orders@Xlibris.com
87884

Dedication

This book is dedicated to my brothers Robert Yarborough and John Yarborough.

My name is Curtis Yarborough. I was born in the state of North Carolina, in a city by the name of Roxboro, which is in Person County. I am the son of Maggie and Willie Prima Yarborough. I am the 6th son and 13th of 14 children. My mother was a homemaker. My father was a sharecropper. My father grew tobacco and other crops, such as corn, okra, tomato, and several types of beans. Tobacco was at that time in North Carolina the major crop. My oldest sister, Estelle, mentioned to me that I was born at the time of cold weather in Roxboro. My father also had a big family of fourteen kids. After the death of my father in 1960, my mother, my brothers and my sisters moved to New York. We moved to the suburb of Mount Vernon, New York. When I became the required age to attend school (kindergarten), I had my first experience of rejection. An older kid made mention to his brother that I had a big head. This younger kid made a loud declaration "He has a big head." I started to look down at my shoes. I was feeling ashamed. I started to walk away, wondering why he said that. I never felt any different from the other children at school. My head size at that time was 6'10". My head was a little bigger than the kids my age (7 years old). From the age of 6, I was made fun of by kids. Most of these kids were African American kids. I never had problems with Caucasians, or other culture children. We moved sometime around the year 1960. My 3 oldest sisters had lived in New York prior. They moved up there seeking employment, moving to Mount Vernon.

Most of the schools in New York or in Mount Vernon were segregated. Some were 90% white, 5% black, 5% other cultures.

Then some were opposite 90% black, 8% white, and 2% other cultures. These schools had worn books, missing pages, outdated and dirty. Two good things about these schools: they had teachers who loved their craft (teaching). Those teachers took their teaching jobs seriously. These teachers at that time had great morals. Christian morals were taught and respected at that time. Prayer and scripture reading were common at that time. Teachers would address issues at that time. They wouldn't tolerate name calling (bad words), cussing, lying, reviling, spitting, fighting, etc.

START OF PERSECUTION

I mentioned earlier that I started to be made fun of at Kindergarten. The first school I attended was Robert Fulton in Mount Vernon. This school was predominantly black. The African American children teased me about my head size. Not all of them, but some of them. The white children never noticed the difference. They treated me with mutual respect. Most of my friends were the white kids or foreign kids, few black youth. Some of the kids called me big head, some called me manhead, and some called me fathead. Some of the young girls called me ugly. Some also said that I had a head like a grown man. When you are 9 years old and your peers say that you have a head like a grown man, it hurts, because you want to be one or at peace with everybody. My head size at that time was 7"1/8. When you look a little different from others, others who are average or referred to as normal would refuse to befriend you. Some of the kids were loud, nasty, and very harsh. I would get mad and try to get into fights with them. The teachers tried to correct those children. In the 1960's, teachers did not tolerate children low rating others because of clothing, physical appearance, speech such as stuttering or wrong pronunciation of words. Teachers had more morals in those days. They had a moral code. There were more Christian morals taught in schools, than what is taught now (2011). When prayer was removed from the school system, all types of ungodly values took over our schools. I was raised to respect older people (elderly folks). Some of the children that I experienced the persecution were not taught to respect the rights of others. Meeting some of their parents reveal to me where these children learned these values. Some New Yorkers were from Southern backgrounds. Some from Alabama, some from North and South Carolina, some from Virginia, some from Mississippi and Georgia, etc. But many of them didn't have the fear of God (Reverence) or respect to God. Some were drug users or alcoholics. My New York upbringing was different from my Southern background.

PARENT POINT ME OUT TO HIS CHILD

I had more than one experience, whereby a father would point me out to his child or children and say "That kid has a big head" or (use the expression) "That kid has a colosso head." Sometimes these parents would break out with laughter. They would encourage their children to make fun of me. They made fun of me. They made me feel like a monster. At times I wish I was dead. Sometimes I wished that I could have done violence to them. I thank God for His mercy; He kept me from suicide, from hurting others physically. I thank God for His unseen hand of protection. Sometimes kids are influenced by others. Some of them are misguided. There are times when they do things out of ignorance, not understanding they are hurting others. Sometimes parents, uncle, cousin, brethren, aunt do not know that it is a sin to revile others. We are the creation of the living God.

BECAUSE OF
THE PERSECUTION

I would not attend sporting events fearing that I would run into people who would make fun of me. I wouldn't eat in the cafeteria or go to study halls. I love basketball and football and other sports, but attending school games was troubling to me. Being in the presence of people who are devaluing you and low rating you can be depressing. I was quick to fight when someone made a negative statement about my head size. When I attended neighborhood parks, I would run into some kids who would refuse to choose me to play with them because they had something against my physical appearance. One kid said to another kid: Do not pick that "Bighead Boy". When somebody did pick me, I played hard to show those who refuse to pick me, that I was a better player than them. Those kids, who picked me to play with them, learned my personality and befriended me. They saw that it was not my head, but what flow out of my heart. I had one encounter with a kid who threw a dodge ball into the side of my head, the crazy thing about this; he was on the same dodge ball team. I was on his side. He holler out "Keep your bighead out of my way" when he threw the ball into my head. I rushed over to him and grabbed him. I tried to fight him. He had no reason to toss the ball at my head. I was side by side him. The gym teacher broke us apart.

MY PARENTS

I mentioned in the beginning of this book that my father died in 1960. I never knew my dad. I never had intimacy with him. My natural father didn't have any direct impact on my life.

We were raised by a single mother. My mother never remarried. She never invited another man into our home. She was a loving and giving person. She loved all her children. Sometimes I mentioned to my mother about some of my experiences (persecutions). She wanted to confront the parents and the children. My mother had righteous indignation. She wanted to fight for me. In my heart, I did not want my mother to confront these people. I always felt I could deal with it. I hid some of my encounters from my mother and my brethren (family) because I knew that they would fight for me. My mother was a friend and an encourager, she loved me. She knew what to say to make me feel bigger in life. She was very tactful. A very patient woman. My mother birth 14 children. She raised 13, one died at birth. The most admirable thing about my mother is that she also raised 5 other children that were not her own. She raised one homeless young white male, and 4 male, and female African American children. She raised them and us on a welfare salary (government benefit), $365.00 a month and the majority of this money went toward rent.She improvise, she made big pots of soup. She would get things from our neighborhood butcher. In the 1960's, butchers would throw away certain parts chicken legs, back, feet, and necks. Butchers now sell what they have thrown away in the past. Now more people consume what they would throw away back in the past. She used what she had to keep us alive. The day my mother transition (died), her natural children and her adoptive children felt a great loss. Claude Russell, my adoptive brother, took her death hard. We will always love him. His love for our mother allows us as her children to know that she was a great woman. She was loving and wasn't partial. She loved her adoptive children with the same love that she had for her own. Going back to me, I had a need for a father. These incidents in my life, made me desire to have a dad speak out for me and to speak up for me. My father died an untimely death. I never saw pictures of him. My sisters and other family members would say I walk like him or speak like him, etc.

WITHOUT A MENTOR

I mentioned I didn't know my father. I never knew him, but I love him. I do not know his characteristics or his actions. My love for him is unconditional. Without him there is no me. I am proud to be his son. I mentioned early that I longed for a father figure to pattern my life after. Without my father DNA (sperm) there is no

Curtis Yarborough or my siblings. Without a mentor or director in life, it can be hard to avoid the pitfalls in life. Without teachers or role models, it would take longer to achieve goals in life. The Bible says behold, children are an inheritance to the Lord, the fruit of the womb a reward (Deuteronomy 28:4). As arrows are in the hand of a warrior (archer) so are the children of one's youth (Psalm127:3, 4). Children bring security and protection. I found a man of the Baptist faith, the Reverend Henry Grant Jones. He was the former pastor of Unity Baptist Tabernacle Church in Mount Vernon. He was a meek and soft spoken man who expressed the love of God. I will always love him. He was a peacemaker and very friendly. If he saw children out of conduct (fighting) he would correct them in love. He walks with a smile and carries himself with integrity. In the public, he walked with humility, behind closed doors I do not know. This preacher displayed the conduct of a Christ like servant. I never saw any unjust actions in his life. He taught me to pattern myself after Jesus the Christ, the Son of the Living God. Without a mentor there is no one to correct the bad directions in life, or habits. Parents and preachers help direct children in life.

DISSECTED FROG IN MY WINTER COAT

I had an incident whereby a kid took a dissected frog and placed it in the pocket of my winter coat. We were in a Biology class and we were being trained to dissect frogs. It was the end of the class. I went and retrieved my coat from the coat rack and I placed one of my arms in the jacket. I entered the other arm and reached for my skull cap that I had worn. I placed my hand in my coat pocket. I felt a cold, wet tough rubber like thing in my pocket. It was that dissected frog. This incident made me mad as hell. If hell can be mad, I was mad. This frog was slimy and smell like alcohol. I looked around the class and I saw this kid laughing. I walked over to him and asked him who put that frog in my pocket. He just smirked. I went over and mentioned it to my teacher. I told her he put that frog in my pocket. She asked me did I see him do it. I said no. She told me if I did not see him do it, I can't blame him for it. I knew he done it. I wanted to kill that boy.

But thanks to God I didn't. I forgave him; he didn't know what he was doing. That was the same kid that made fun of my head. I had another incident whereby this 12 year old girl painted the side of my head with water paint. "Hey, I painted bighead head." her expression. I started a fight with her. She scratched me in my face. The teacher stopped us from fighting. I thought if I lived at peace with others or did right to others I would not experience what I experienced. I notice that if you look different from others or express yourself differently, it brings about persecution. My favorite winter coat was contaminated by that nasty frog. I never had anything to do with that kid again.

ACCEPTING BUYOUT PROGRAM/SEEKING NEW EMPLOYMENT

In the year 1999, I was seeking employment. Lexington Furniture was laying off. I took the buyout program that LFI was offering. I had a choice of being transferred to one of the other plants. But I chose to take the retirement package. I went to the employment office in High Point. A job counselor sent me on an interview for a job. This job was at a particular furniture company. I am not going to expose the company, but it was a well known company. I believe the interview was on Tuesday around 9 am or 10 am. I am not sure of the time. I walked in the furniture business and walked up to the receptionist. She asked me who I came to see. I informed her that I had a job interview. She asked me to fill out an application. She contacted the supervisor. The supervisor came out of the office and asked me to follow him. I followed him through the building. We went through a room of about 50 to 70 workers. He took me in a small office. He asked me to sit down. He explained to me what type of wood products they produced. He then told me about the company benefits, sick days, holidays, bonuses, etc. He gave me a history of the company. Then he surprised me with this statement, "You won't like it here." I asked why? He did not fully explain but said to me that they are going to make fun of you. Most of the workers were young and black. That supervisor knew the environment when he made that statement. I wonder who he was talking about. I could have filed a discrimination charge with a lawyer and sue that company. I walked out not mad, but confused not fully understanding why that supervisor made that statement. The supervisor was white (Caucasian). I was 41 years old. That supervisor did not give me a clear explanation. I guess it was the bighead. My 7"1/4 head. God made me into what He desires me to be. I am not ashamed of what my Creator allowed me to be. I love me and most of all God loves me. Men evaluation of me, do not bring praises or honor to God. Only God's evaluation of me counts. I left that supervisor knowing that God has the last say about my life. The next week I found a better job with better pay than the one I applied for. This is an imperfect world. We came into a world that has corrupted through sin. Sin means missing the mark. There was a standard that the Creator of the universe set for His Creation. He told the first man and woman not to eat the fruit of the tree. Their disobedience brought a curse on the world system. Our lives have been changed because of Adam and Eve. Romans 5:17-21.For if by one man's offence, death reigned by one, much more they which receive abundance of grace and of the gift of righteousness shall reign in life by one Jesus Christ. Therefore as by the offense of one, judgment came upon all men to condemnation even so by the righteousness of one the free gift came upon all men unto the justification of life. For as by one man's disobedience many were made sinners, so by the obedience of one shall many be made righteous. More over the law entered, that the offence might abound, but where sin abounded, grace did much more abound, that as sin hath reigned unto death, even so might grace reign through righteousness unto eternal life by Jesus Christ our Lord. Quotes from Romans 5:17-21 NKJ and KJV. For if by the one man's offense, death reined through the one, much more those who receive abundance of grace and of the gift of righteousness will reign in life through the one Jesus Christ. There as through one man's righteous act the free gift came to all men, resulting in justification of life for as by one man disobedience many were made sinners, so also by one man's obedience many will be made righteous. Moreover the law entered that the offense might abound. But where sin abounded grace might reign through righteousness in eternal life through Jesus Christ Our Lord. Romans 5:17-21

THINGS THAT OFFEND ME

There are things that offend me in these days. I watch people with severe and body burns made fun of. We live in a day where pride has invaded the hearts of man to make them think that calamity can't happen to them. Fire in homes, scalding hot water knock over off a stove on a child or an adult can cause lifetime scars. We should walk with humility knowing that if it wasn't for the grace of God, there I go. The same thing with outward appearance, it is only temporal on this earth. The Bible talks about those who serve Jesus would be blessed with new and approve body (Glorified Body). I have seen people who were born with 6 fingers and 6 toes, also people born without legs and without arms. Sometimes parents of children use environmental toxins, not knowing the indirect effect. I was watching The Tyra Banks Show, Tyra had a woman who loves to eat chalk, chalkboard chalk. She was pregnant and she ate baby powder.

This woman does not know the negative effects that these substances would have on her baby and her own body. It can cause the body (DNA) to deform or mutilate. These components can change the body mechanism to produce healthy organs; such as eyes, nose, teeth, etc. These substances can keep the body from protecting itself. Many times we hear of couples having some kids that have defects, Cerebral Palsy and other birth defects or diseases. Some things are caused by home cleaning products. My heart goes out to a story in the Bible where a bunch of youth reviled a holy man of God. This man of God named Elijah walked close with Jehovah God. He was a praying man who had the favor and power of God on his life. As Elijah left Jericho he went toward Bethel, a city in Israel. II kings 2:23. King James Version and he went up from thence unto Bethel; and as he was going by the way, there came forth little children out of the city, and mocked him, and said unto him, Go up, thou bald head. Go up, thou bald head. Verse 24 and he turned back, and looked on them, and cursed them in the name of the Lord. And there came forth two she bears out of the woods, and tore forty and two children of them. This is the New King James Version verse 23. Then he went up from Jericho to Bethel–and as he was going up the road, some youths came from the city and mocked him, and said to him "Go up you bald head", "Go up, you bald head". Verse 24, so he turned around and looked at them and pronounced a curse on them in the name of the Lord. And two female bears came out of the woods and mauled forty-two of the youths. Verse 25, then he went from there to Mt. Carmel, and from there he returned to Samaria. God is displeased when we make fun of the handicap. God opposes those who walk in pride and arrogance. Good looks are a gift from God. Good and attractive physical appearance does not grant you more favor with God. A meek and a peaceful spirit in the sight of God are of much value. James 4:6

But He gives more grace (unmerited favor) to those who walk in humility. Therefore, He says, God resists the proud but He gives grace to the humble. This word grace means favor, unmerited favor. You do not have to do anything to earn it. Unconditional affection toward someone. If you do research on Elijah, he was a bald head man. These children were devaluing the man of God by their actions. It brought judgment to these children. God gets displeasure when we defame one another or low rate each other with our mouths. That is why coarse joking is a sin. II Corinthians 6;11

LOVING FAMILY

My sister Ruby loved me. She was a sister who always felt that she should give you advice. She always gave me advice about my hygiene. She cared about my physical appearance, health, and hygiene was important to her. She would take offense if anybody did anything to offend me. She would often speak what was on her mind.

She was very opinionated. One incident that comes to my mind. I was 8 years old. I drank or ate something that gave me the runs (diarrhea). The school nurse called my house and talked to my mother. My mother informed my sister that I had gotten sick at school. My mother asked my sister to go to the school house to find out what had happened to me. I will always treasure that moment. You might ask me why? Ruby came to the school and cleaned me up. She brought clean clothes from home. I was messed up and had a headache and sour stomach. My sister Curley Mae loves me and is truly a woman who believes in you doing your best. She is very frank and upfront. She always speaks her mind. She cares about how I dress, my hygiene, my health, what I eat, and how much I sleep. She is truly a great sister. I will always love her. She is a sister who gave me life checks. She is always concerned about how I live. She is a person that I don't mind giving an account to. She makes sure that I am living right and doing right. She taught me how to tie ties, shirt ties (neckties). She is a blessing. My 2 youngest sisters are Thelma and Marie who are ministers of the gospel. They have been encouragers of Christian ethics. My brother Willie is a thinker and problem solver. He is mechanically inclined. He is a person that pushes me to excellence. I love discussing computers and playing Chess with him. He is a great brother and always gives me sound advice. My sister Estelle is a woman who can give family members their ages and their family lineage. She always cares about my well being, health, and physical appearance. When I was 14, she tried to teach me sex (facts and myths). The birds and bees, flowers and trees. She tried to instruct me on street morals. I will always love her. Cornell and Tommy are brothers who showed me how to take care of their families. They served faithful on their jobs, retired with honor. I gave a summary of my brethren and how they helped to contribute to my development.

Now I want to go back to my topic "Hey Bighead". I was reviled from kindergarten and at times I still get nasty comments made toward me. Wiki-dictionary states the word revile comes from a French word formed from "vil" which is also the root word "vile" which means wicked. This word means to use abusive or contemptuous names. It also means to disregard. All the insults, all the reviling, being looked down upon because of the size of my head. It did not make feel less of a person. I know that the Creator of Life loves me. I love myself. God's love is greater than any human love. Human love has its limitations. God's love is everlasting. Human love is conditional. It is based upon what you can do for that person. God's love is without merit. It will never die or end. Man's love is based on what you do for them or what they can acquire from you. God's love is unconditional. He loves you regardless of your shortcomings. He loves our ethnicity, the color of our skin, the articulation of our speech. Your imperfection does not keep Him from loving you.

FIVE SENSES VERSUS PHYSICAL APPEARANCE

We take the five senses of the body for granted. Without eyesight, we can't see the things in front of us, or on the side of us, or above or beneath us. Without the ability to see, we can't enjoy the beautiful colors God made in life. Without ears and the ability to hear sounds, we wouldn't be able to communicate with words. Being able to hear can protect us from harm, falling objects, runaway vehicles, dog attacks, animal attacks, fire alarms, telephone calls, etc.

Touching allows us to examine a thing. To be aware of with the sense of touch.

TASTE

To be able to find out the flavor of something by taking a little into the mouth. Ability to be able to recognize sweet, sour, bitter, or salty flavors. With this sense, we are able to know what is acceptable to the body.

SMELL

To become aware of the odor of by means of sense organs located in the nose. Without smell, we couldn't detect harmful odors, germs, or toxins you can't function at your best living without all these senses. You can function in life without being handsome or beautiful. Life is made difficult without these five senses.

Theses senses are important. Good looks are important to the bearer or the one who is attractive to the displayer of the physical looks. I believe everyone wants to be attractive or feel attractive. There are many who killed themselves because they didn't look a certain way. Some women desire wider hips, bigger breasts, or smaller ones. Some want bigger buttocks and in reverse. I heard of women in New York who have had 50 operations to change different parts of their body. I am not against people who use wigs, face lifts, breast reduction, or use cellulite machines to remove fat or dentistry or hair grafts, etc. Whatever is safe and can improve your appearance I do not think that God is against. When you go in excess. When you worship your physical outlook or appearance and forget who made you. It is the Spirit of God we ought to worship.

Earlier in the book, there was a typographical error in reference to my father's name. My father's correct name was Willie Primer Yarborough.

I thank God for making me. I see many people who blame God for not making them physically attractive or highly intelligent or rich or a famous athlete or a movie star. We live in a generation or time whereby people can hire doctors to change or alter any part of the body. The nose, face, neck, legs, buttocks, breasts, etc. can be altered or changed. Michael Jackson changed his nose and his skin tone. Many actors, politicians, entertainers have changed their appearance. I am not ashamed of the way God made me. I am not mad at the Creator of life. He chose to allow me to be born in the manner that I am. I am the only child of my parents whose head is what some feel is abnormal. All of my brethren have what some call normal size heads. They look at me as the water head child. God has made me wonderful. I might have a head that is not proportion to my body but I walk in humility knowing that God loves me. Most of all I love me. God has named me his son, the fruits of his thoughts. He knew me before the foundation of this world. My name is King Curtis, the son of the living God.

Most sickness and disease are cause by depression associated with stress. When we focus on the opinions of others, we bring about low self esteem, we stop creation in our lives we do not fulfill what the creator of life design us to be. We are all call to fulfill a task we were created to introduce the king of kings, the lord of lords. We were called to fulfill a vocation. JEREMIAH 29:11 for I know the thoughts that I think toward you, says the lord, thoughts of peace and not of evil, to give you a future and a hope.

Made in the USA
Las Vegas, NV
29 January 2022

42581077R00033